THE LIVING EINSTEIN

The Stephen Hawking Story
Biography Kids Books
Children's Biography Books

DISSECTED LIVES
auto biographies

Speedy Publishing LLC

40 E. Main St. #1156

Newark, DE 19711

www.speedypublishing.com

Copyright 2017

Stephen Hawking is a scientist and astrophysicist. He was born on January 8, 1942 and he is best known for the book A Brief History of time as well as his work known as Hawking radiation. In this book, you will learn about his life and accomplishments.

HIS EARLY YEARS

Stephen William Hawking was born on January 8, 1942 in Oxford, England. He was raised with a very highly educated family. Both his mother and father attended Oxford University and Frank, his father, was a medical researcher.

Oxford University

Oxford University

He enjoyed science and math while in school and earned his nickname "Einstein". While he wanted to study math at Oxford, he didn't have a math degree and he decided to take chemistry and physics instead.

He found the coursework at college to be quite easy, and enjoyed classical music and he also decided to become a member of the school's boat club. After he graduated, he decided to go to Cambridge to obtain his PhD.

Cambridge University

Cambridge University

HIS ALS DIAGNOSIS

He started to have health issues while studying at Cambridge University for his PhD. He became quite clumsy, falling and dropping items for no apparent reason, and his speech started to become slurred. After going through many tests, his doctors found out that he had a disease known as ALS (also known as Lou Gehrig's Disease). His doctor told him at that time that he might only live for a few years.

OVERCOMING ALS

While Hawking initially was depressed with this diagnosis, he decided there were things he would like to accomplish during his life. He started studying and working harder than before. He was determined to get his PhD before his death. About this same time, he met Jane Wilde, and fell in love with her. Between his love for Jane and his desire to work and get his PhD, he had a reason to live.

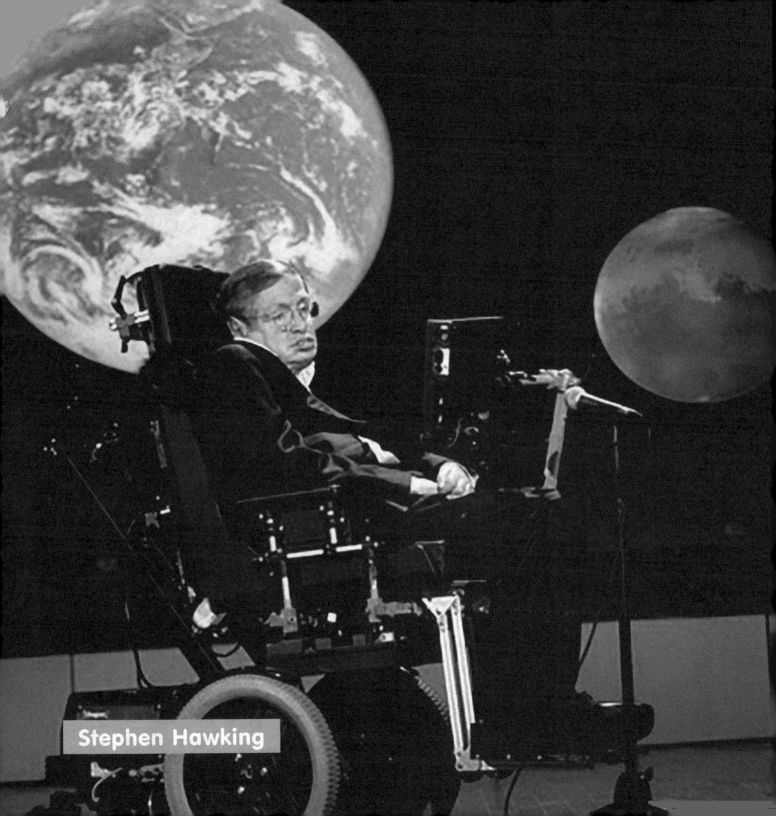

Stephen Hawking

In spite of the initial poor diagnosis he received from the doctors, he has gone on to live a full and productive life with the assistance of modern medicine and science. While he is confined to the wheelchair and is unable to talk, he is able to communicate with a voice synthesizer and a touch pad computer.

HIS MARRIAGES AND CHILDREN

Hawking married Jane Wilde on July 14, 1965 and they proceeded to have three children; Robert, born in May of 1967, Lucy, born in 1970, and Timothy, born in April of 1979. Their marriage ended in divorce in 1995.

Stephen Hawking

Stephen Hawking School

Hawking then proceeded to marry one of his nurses, Elaine Mason. After this marriage, his family began to feel excluded and thought he was being abused physically.

However, he refused to make a complaint and the police investigations were subsequently closed. They quietly divorced in 2006. He has resumed a close relationship with his ex-wife Jane, as well as his children and grandchildren.

Black holes

HAWKING RADIATION AND BLACK HOLES

Stephen has spent a lot of academic work in researching space-time theories and black holes. He has written many papers of importance on this subject and is known to be a noted expert on the subject of relativity and black holes. His most famous discovery, perhaps, was his demonstration that black holes emit some radiation. Before this, it was believed that the black holes were not able to become smaller since nothing can escape their enormous gravity. The radiation from the black holes is now known as Hawking Radiation.

A BRIEF HISTORY OF TIME

He also enjoyed spending time writing books. He published A Brief History of Time in 1988. It covered modern subjects on cosmology including the big bang and black holes in terms that the average reader would be able to understand. It became very popular and sold millions of copies as well as remaining on the best-seller list of the London Sunday Times for four years. It only contained one equation, Einstein's famous $E = mc2$.

Black holes

典藏版

A Brief History of Time book

Since then he has written several more books that include A Briefer History in Time, On the Shoulders of Giants, as well as The Universe in a Nutshell.

Hawking has also co-authored many children's books with Lucy, his daughter, including George and the Big Bang and George's Cosmic Treasure Hunt.

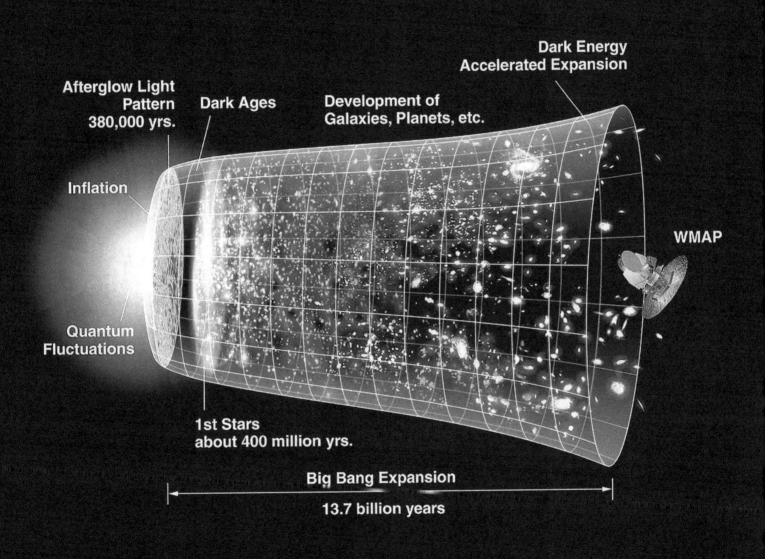

POPULAR MEDIA APPEARANCES

At the party for the release of his home video version of A Brief History of Time, Leonard Nimoy, from the cast of Star Trek, heard that Stephen wanted to appear on the show. Nimoy made the required contact and Stephen was cast to play himself as a holographic simulation, in 1993 during an episode of Star Trek: The Next Generation. That same year, his synthesizer voice became recorded for a Pink Floyd song titled "Keep Talking", as well as a 1999 appearance on The Simpsons.

He also appeared in the documentaries The Real Stephen Hawking in 2001, Stephen Hawking: Profile, in 2002, and Hawking in 2013, as well as the documentary series in 2008 titled Stephen Hawking, Master of the Universe. He also made guest appearances on Futurama and The Big Bang Theory. He permitted use of his copyrighted voice in the 2014 biographical film The Theory of Everything, where Eddie Redmayne portrayed him in an award-winning role. In 2014, he was featured in Monty Python Live (Mostly).

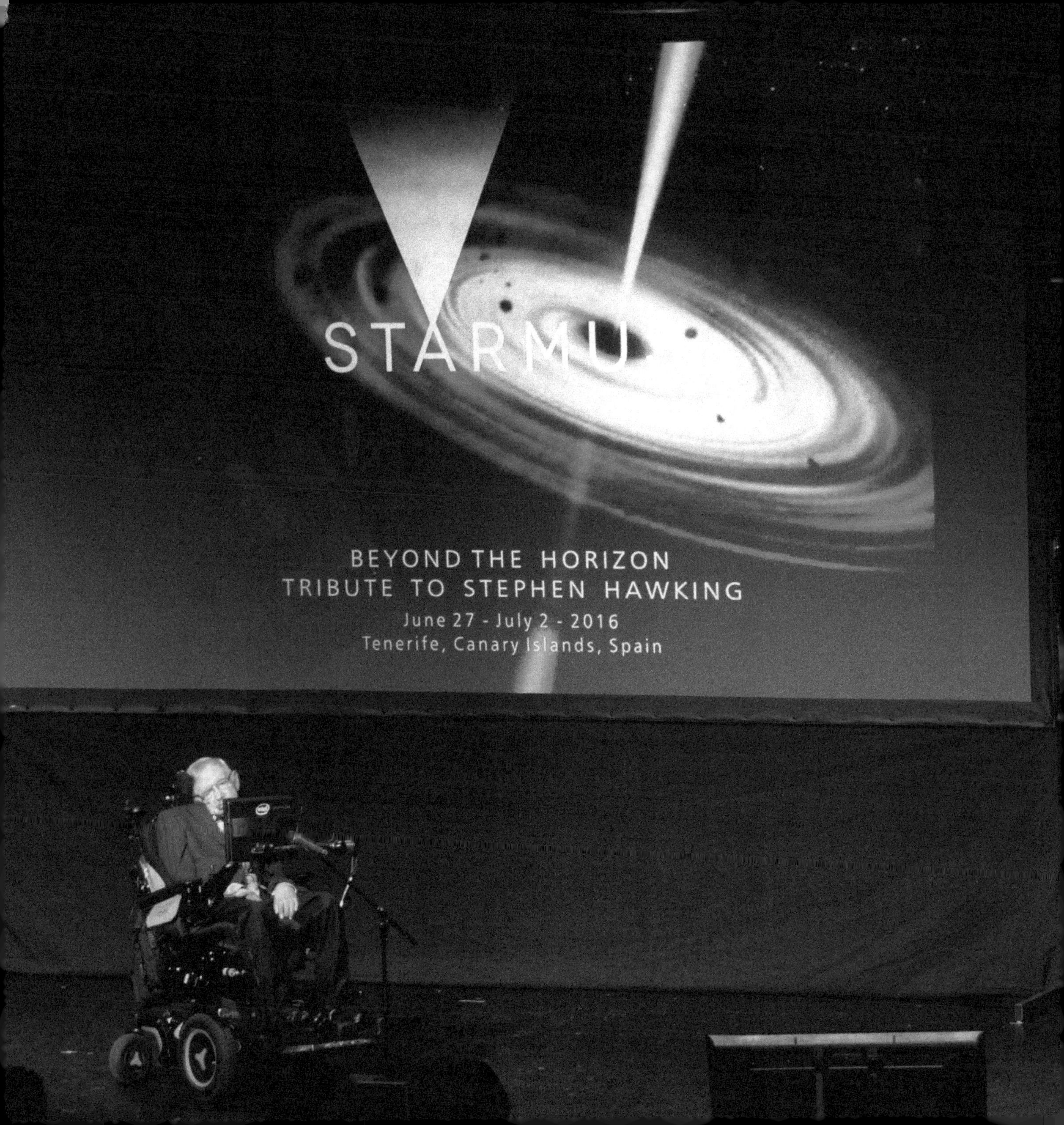
STARMUS
BEYOND THE HORIZON
TRIBUTE TO STEPHEN HAWKING
June 27 - July 2 - 2016
Tenerife, Canary Islands, Spain

Black Holes

WHAT IS A BLACK HOLE?

The black holes are one of the more powerful and mysterious forces of the universe. A black hole occurs when gravity becomes so strong that nothing around it, not even light, can escape. Its mass is so dense that the gravity's force is too strong that light cannot even escape.

ARE WE ABLE TO SEE THEM?

They are truly invisible. We actually cannot see black holes since they do not reflect light. By observing light and objects around the black holes, scientists know they exist. Strange things happening around the black holes has to do with space time and quantum physics which makes them popular subjects for science fiction, even though they are very real.

Black Holes

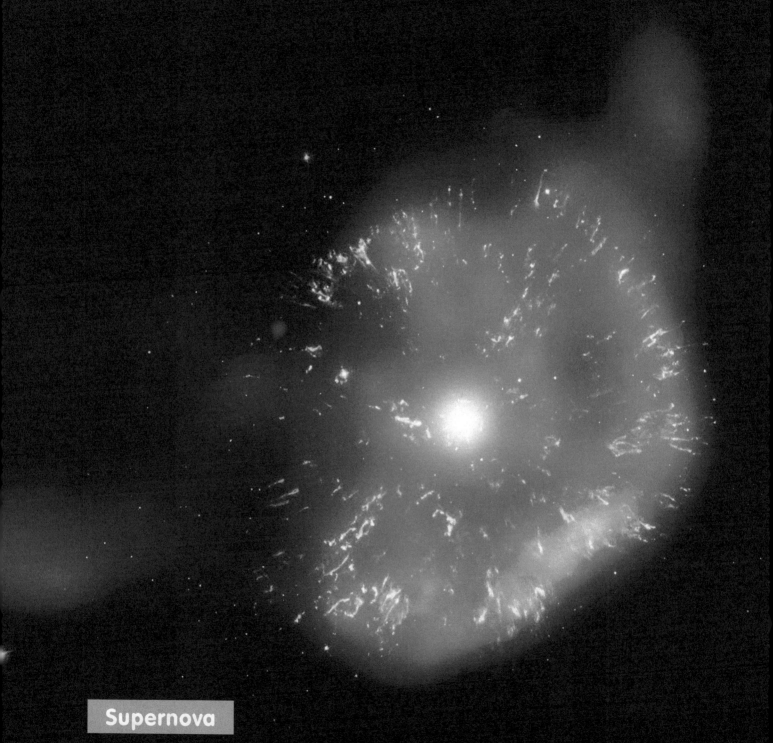
Supernova

HOW DO BLACK HOLES FORM?

When giant stars are at the end of the lifecycles, they explode and form into black holes. This is known as a supernova. The star will collapse down into a very small size if it has enough mass. Due to its enormous mass and small size, the gravity becomes so strong that it absorbs light and becomes a black hole. It is possible for a black hole to grow to an incredibly large size as they continue absorbing light and mass. They can also absorb additional stars. Several scientists believe there are super-massive black holes at the center of the galaxies.

EVENT HORIZON

A special boundary surrounding a black hole is known as an event horizon. At this point everything, including light, must go towards the black hole. Once you have crossed the event horizon, there is no escape!

Event Horizon

WHO DISCOVERED THE BLACK HOLE?

Originally proposed in the 18th century, the idea of it was originally proposed by two different scientists: Pierre-Simon Laplace and John Michell. John Archibald Wheeler came up with the name "black hole" in 1967.

WHAT IS GRAVITY?

This is the force that mysteriously makes everything fall towards the earth.

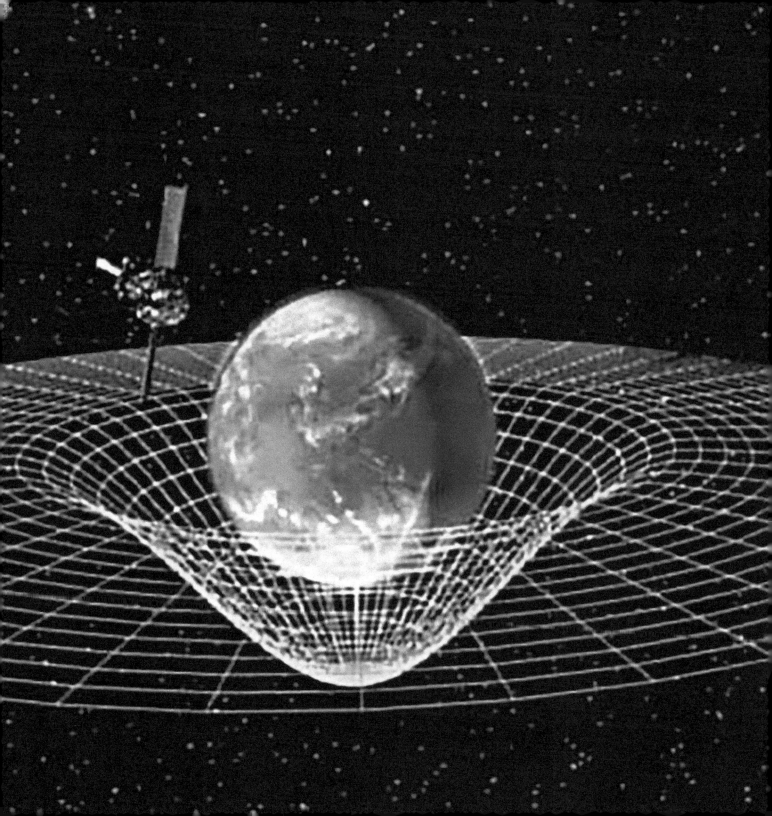

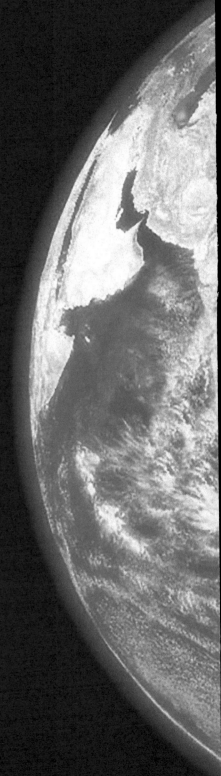

All objects have gravity, but some objects, such as the Sun and the Earth, have a lot more than the others.

Earth

The size of the object decides how much gravity pull is has, or more specifically, its mass. It is also dependent upon how near you are to an object. The closer you are to the object, the stronger the pull of the gravity will be.

GRAVITATION ON EARTH

Earth's gravity

WHY IS GRAVITY IMPORTANT?

It is quite important in our daily life. Without the gravity pull of the Earth, we would fly off of it. We would need to strapped to it. When you kick a ball, it would fly off and never be found. While it sounds like fun, we most certainly would not able to live without it.

On a bigger scale, it is also important. The gravity of the Sun keeps the Earth in orbit around it. On Earth, life needs the light and warmth of the Sun for survival. Gravity also helps keep Earth the correct distance from the Sun, so that it is not too cold or too hot.

Isaac Newton

WHO DISCOVERED GRAVITY?

The first person that dropped a heavy item on their foot probably knew something was happening, but it was first described mathematically by a scientist known as Isaac Newton. This theory is referred to as Newton's Law of Universal Gravitation. In his theory of relativity, Albert Einstein later made some improvement on Newton's theory.

WEIGHT

Gravity's force upon an object is weight. On Earth our weight is the amount of force the gravity pull of the Earth has on us and how hard its pulling us to the surface.

Gravity waves in the binary system

DO OBJECTS FALL AT THE SAME SPEED?

The answer to that question is yes, and this is known as the equivalence principle. Objects with different masses will fall at the same speed to the Earth. If you have two balls with different masses and drop them from the top of a building, they will strike the ground at the same time.

For additional information about Stephen Hawking and his works you can go to your local library, research the internet, and ask questions of your teachers, family and friends.

YSICS

Visit

DISSECTED LIVES
auto biographies

www.DissectedLives.Com

To download more inspiring autobiographies and biographies
of great people from our website. Discover more about people
that changed the world during their time!

Visit our website to download more
Free eBooks and Get Discount Codes!

CPSIA information can be obtained
at www.ICGtesting.com
Printed in the USA
JSHW021047131222
PP12154600001B/1